OLYMPIC GOLD

Edited by Nicole Carmichael

Written by Philippa Perry

WORLD BOOK / TWO-CAN

OLYMPIC GOLD

First published in the United States in 1996
by World Book Inc.
525 W. Monroe
20th Floor
Chicago
IL USA 60661
in association with Two-Can Publishing Ltd.

Copyright © Two-Can Publishing Ltd 1996

**For information on other World Book products,
call 1-800-255-1750, x 2238.**

ISBN 0-7166-1735-8 (pbk.)
LC: 96-60466

Printed in Hong Kong

1 2 3 4 5 6 7 8 9 10 99 98 97 96

Design by Simon Relph. Picture research by Sam Riley and Dipika Parmar Jenkins. Production by Joya Bart-Plange.
Front cover photographs: Zefa Pictures. Inserts: Popperfoto: bl. Sporting Pictures: bc&br.

Picture credits: Allsport: 6/7c, br, 9l, br, 10/11c, 11r, 13cr, br, 15br, 17br, 21br, 22cl, 23br, 26c, 27tl, 28bl, 29tr, 30, Allsport/Hulton Deutsch: 12l&bc, 20, 29br. Colorsport: 6tl, 8l, 17t, 19tr, bl, br, 22/23c, 23tr, 24c, 25tr. Hulton Deutsch: 5bl, 8tl, 13tcl. Mary Evans: 4c, 19tl, The Ronald Grant Archive; 8br. Popperfoto: 9tr, 10cl, 14tl, 15tl, 18tr, bc, 23ct, 24bl, 24/25c, 28tc. Sporting Pictures (UK) Ltd: 7tr, 14b 16b, 17bl, 18 tl, 21tr, bl, 24tc, 27tr, br, 28tl.

Illustrations: Bernard Long: 4/5, Chris West: 28.

CONTENTS

▲ *The first Olympic champion, Coroibos the cook*

▲ *Thankfully, not all events have stayed the same.*

Let the games BEGIN

The Olympics were all Greek to the first athletes!

When we watch the modern Olympic Games, with their high-tech stadiums, satellite TV links, and computer scoring systems, it's hard to believe it all started thousands of years ago in a green valley in ancient Greece.

Athletics played a vital part in the religious festivals of the ancient Greeks. People believed that their gods were pleased by mortals competing against each other in physical games. Some tribes and cities

▼ *The site of the ancient Olympic Games in Olympia, Greece*

even held religious festivals every four years to honor their gods.

The festival at Olympia was held in honor of the king of the gods, Zeus. Situated in western Greece, Olympia was an open space with temples and shrines. The games there were held outside this central religious area at a special stadium and race track.

EARLY EVENTS

The first Olympic Games on record were held in 776 B.C. (although it's thought that they could date back to 1370 B.C.). At that time there was just one event–a sprint over a distance of around 200 yards. A swift-footed cook named Coroibos was the hero of the 776 B.C. Olympic Games, and the whole festival was over in just a day!

Winning was everything in the ancient Olympics, and there was no such thing as second or third place. But there wasn't a gold medal for the prize winner to treasure, just a simple crown made from the leaves of the sacred olive tree.

HEAVY METAL
Later, five days were allowed for the Games and other events were added, such as spectacular chariot races where teams of horses charged furiously around a circular course. There was also bareback horse-riding and running races similar to modern athletics competitions. But there was one big difference – athletes had to run in full armor! An event called the pentathlon, which consisted of five stages, was to form the basis for the modern heptathlon and decathlon.

DYING TO ENTERTAIN
As the Games became more and more popular, the audiences clamored for greater thrills and spills. They got them in 648 B.C. when a brutal and deadly sport called pancratium was added to the Games. This consisted of a vicious mixture of wrestling, boxing with spiked gloves, and judo, with punching and kicking allowed.

Not surprisingly, athletes often died taking part in it.

Once the Roman Empire had conquered Greece, the games lost their religious purpose. Contestants in the Games became interested only in winning money. After standards started to plummet, Emperor Theodosius put an end to the Games in A.D. 394.

Women were first allowed to compete in the Olympic Games in 1912.

HISTORY REPEATED
It wasn't until 1,502 years later that the Olympic Games made a long-awaited comeback. In 1875 a group of German archaeologists discovered the ruined site of the ancient Games. This gave a Frenchman named Baron de Coubertin the idea of holding a modern Olympic Games.

The first new-style Games included many of the sports of the ancient Games but with added new events, such as the grueling marathon race.

The first modern Olympic Games took place in 1896 in Athens. They were set up to encourage world peace and friendship and to promote amateur athletics. Only 13 countries took part, and all the contestants were men.

The next Games, held in 1900, turned out to be a complete failure. The events were badly organized, and some athletes competing didn't even know it was the Olympics!

Plans were soon underway to make sure that future Olympic Games would be very special.

▲ *"The most important thing in the Olympic Games is not winning but taking part."* *So said the man who revived the games, Baron de Coubertin (second from left).*

▲ *Countries compete against each other to create the biggest and best-equipped stadiums to stage the Olympics. The Japanese spent five years getting ready for the 1964 Tokyo Games. They spent $2.8 billion and built a beautiful stadium, a 17-story hotel, expressway, and high-tech Olympic village for the athletes.*

The spectacular opening ceremonies of the modern Olympic Games have become almost as popular as the events themselves. No Olympic Games would be complete without the lighting of the Olympic flame. Runners in cross-country relays carry a lighted torch from the valley of Olympia, Greece, to the stadium where the games are to be held. Thousands of athletes take part, and it's a great honor to be selected to carry the torch on its journey over mountains and seas to the Olympic stadium. The final lucky runner circles the track and lights the Olympic flame, which is kept burning throughout the Games.

The longest torch relay within one country was for the 1988 Winter Games in Canada.

GET SET, *GO!*

The scene is set for a winning experience

The torch arrived from Greece on Nov. 17, 1987, and was then transported 11,228 miles by foot, aircraft, snowmobile, and dogsled until it reached Calgary on February 13, 1988.

FAN-TASTIC

At one of the first Olympics, in Paris in 1900, there were more athletes than spectators – only 1,000 people turned up! Today several million people go to the Games, and millions more enjoy them on TV.

The Games always begin with an impressive parade. The athletes march into the stadium, with the Greeks leading the way, followed by the other countries' athletes in alphabetical order. After the head of state of the host country declares the Games open, the Olympic flag is raised. Its five interlocking rings represent the different continents of the world.

SPECTACULAR

There have been many magnificent opening ceremonies. The Norwegians pulled out all the stops in 1994 in an incredible display on ice and snow in Lillehammer at the largest Winter Games ever staged. And show biz came to the Olympics with an all-singing and dancing spectacle at the Los Angeles Games in 1984. At the Moscow Olympics in 1980, the center of the athletic stadium was full of people forming the word "Welcome" in big letters, while thousands of balloons were released into the air.

Every four years the opening ceremonies get more and more lavish, records are broken, and spectacular feats are achieved – and that's before the Games even begin!

GOLDEN WONDER

however, the French were determined to go one better. Winners at the Paris Games in 1900 cruised home with solid gold medals for the first and only time in Olympic history.

WHAT? NO MEDALS?

Some years there weren't any medals at all, and athletes had to be content with special prizes, such as a piece of art or a statue. Hardly the same as glittering "gold" medals!

From 1928 the medal design stayed the same until the Barcelona Games in 1992 when a Spanish sculptor was asked to design new medals. He decided to use a bit more gold and added the Olympic rings and laurel leaves. But even if the medals were made of tin, they'd still be worth their weight in gold!

Congratulations – you've won copper! Everyone knows that the Olympic medals are made of gold, silver, and bronze. But are they? In fact, the gold medal is made of silver plated with gold, the silver medal is silver, and the bronze is made of mostly copper.

At the early modern Games in Athens in 1896, the organizers decided that it would be too flashy to award solid gold medals to the winners. So winning athletes had to make do with medals made of silver. On one side the medals showed the Greek god Zeus holding Victory, the goddess of sport, on a globe. The flip side showed a view of the ancient Greek building, the Parthenon, on the Acropolis.

At the next Olympics,

Simply THE BEST

Record breakers and history's heroes

◄ SEASONED WINNERS

The only man to win a gold medal in both the Summer and Winter Games was American Edward Patrick Francis Egan. He boxed his way to the top in the light heavyweight title in 1920. Then he squeezed into the four-man bobsled team at the 1932 Lake Placid Winter Olympics and cruised to gold again!

▲ PERFECT 10

At the 1976 Montreal Games, the 14-year-old Romanian gymnast Nadia Comaneci stepped out to make Olympic history. More than 18,000 spectators watched in amazement as she was awarded a perfect 10 score on the asymmetrical bars. In the same Games she notched up six more perfect scores.

► ME TARZAN!

Johnny Weissmuller made a big splash at the Paris Games in 1924 and the Amsterdam Olympics in 1928 – he ended up swimming away with eight gold medals! He later became the first Olympic winner to dive into a Hollywood starring role.

▲ TIDAL WAVE

American swimmer Mark Spitz predicted he would take home six medals from the 1968 Olympics, but only swam away with two. However, he was the shining star of the swimming events at the 1972 games in Munich. He went home with a record seven gold medals for individual and team events!

▼ MARATHON MAN

Running without track shoes, Abebe Bikila from Ethiopia became the first man in history to win two consecutive Olympic marathons. After crossing the finishing line in 1964 in the fastest time ever, he still had some energy left to entertain the crowd with exercises!

◄ GOLD DISCS

Al Oerter became a legend in athletics. The dynamic discus thrower was the first athlete to win four gold medals in consecutive Olympics – 1956, 1960, 1964, and 1968.

THE YOUNG ONES

Some Olympic champions have struck gold at an age when most children are still at school

The Olympic Games test the best athletes in their sport. Whether you're 15 or 55, there's no upper or lower age-limit to take part. However, the rules state that people must be able to compete without damaging their health. If athletes are too old or too young they may be putting their bodies and minds under too much pressure.

GYM KIDS

Some of the youngest athletes at any Olympics can be found in the gymnastics arena. In fact, most world-class gymnasts have retired before the age that the rest of the world starts working!

As competition in gymnastics became fiercer during the '60s and '70s, gymnastic coaches began to look for younger and younger children, who had the agility and lack of fear to give breathtaking performances.

Olga Korbut (above right) was one of the most famous and popular gymnasts of all time. She was just nine years old when she started

training every day at a gymnastics club in Russia. By the time she was 14 she was a national star.

Nadia Comaneci trained intensively for years. Her talent was spotted at school when she was just six. After that she attended the National Institute of Gymnastics in Romania, where she was given free meals, accommodations, training, equipment, and school lessons.

American Mary Lou Retton (above, center) was sixteen when she won gold at the Los Angeles Olympics in 1984. She took part in her first major national competition when she was only eight years old.

Coaches often scout out budding gymnasts when they are just five years old.

SURPRISE PRIZE

The youngest male gold medalist in history hadn't planned to compete at all! Amazingly, he went home from the Paris Olympics in 1900 with gold in his pocket and a great big smile on his face.

Dr. Hermanus Brockmann was supposed to cox the coxed-pair race for the Netherlands, but had to withdraw from the event as he was too heavy for the boat. Therefore, a young French boy was asked to step into his seat, and the team went on to win the

gold medal. Although no one knows his name or his exact age (which was between 7 and 10 years old), the boy went down in the record books as the youngest Olympic champion.

The youngest female champion was Kim Yoon-Mi from South Korea. She was just 13 years old when she won gold in the 3,000-meter short-track speed skating relay event in 1994. This was an incredible achievement, considering the power and training that speed skaters need.

TEEN SPIRIT
● TOP TEN
Bob Mathias (above left) was just 17 when he grabbed gold in the decathlon at the 1948 London Olympics. He dominated the event for many years and then went on to hurdle some tricky political issues when he became a U.S. congressman.

● RELAY ON ME
The youngest track and field gold medalist was the American runner Barbara Jones, who competed in the winning 4-x-100-meter relay at the Helsinki Olympics in 1952. She was just 15 years old when her Olympic dream came true.

● SLIDE SHOW
You've got to be slightly reckless to enjoy hurtling around a chute of sheer ice. So perhaps being young might help. American William Fiske, the driver of the winning four-man bobsled team, was just 16 when he went for gold at the 1928 Winter Olympics.

LEGENDS OF THE

The tension mounts, the athletes are on the starting blocks, and the starter's gun rips the air

There's nothing like the atmosphere of the Olympic running track. In seconds and minutes, dreams become reality or are shattered forever. But some track performances have gone down in history, never to be forgotten.

▲ HAROLD ABRAHAMS
Nationality: **British**
Event: **100 m**
Harold Abrahams earned his place in the history books when he trained with more dedication than any athlete before him to win gold in the 100 meters. At the Paris Olympics in 1924 he proved that maximum fitness and intensive training do pay off. You may have seen the movie

Chariots of Fire, which was all about Harold Abrahams and the other athletes who earned gold for Britain at the 1924 Games.

▼ DORANDO PIETRI
Nationality: **Italian**
Event: **marathon**
The marathon is one of the most grueling races in the Games. Competitors have to run a course of over 26 miles in any weather. In London in 1908 Dorando Pietri, from Italy, led the marathon right up to the finish in the stadium. Then, with the finish in sight he collapsed from exhaustion and had to be carried over the finish line on a stretcher.

Although he didn't win the race, his strength and courage made him a public hero.

▶ JESSE OWENS
Nationality: **American**
Event: **100 m, 200 m, and long jump**
Jesse Owens stands out from the rest of the Olympic field because of his amazing achievements. At the Berlin Olympics in 1936 he won the dream triple, the 100 and 200 meters, and the long jump.

Owens's win was even more triumphant considering that Adolf Hitler (Germany's fascist leader at the time) dictated that black people were inferior to white people. The arena was filled with swastikas, the fascist emblem, and hostility toward the black athletes was everywhere. But Owens triumphed over the hatred and won the day.

TRACK

▲ FANNY BLANKERS-KOEN
Nationality: **Dutch**
Event: **100 m, 200 m, 4-x-100-m relay, and 100-m hurdles**
Fanny Blankers-Koen of the Netherlands was one of the greatest women athletes of all time. When she was just 18, she was selected for the Berlin Games in 1936, but failed to win a medal. Because of World War II she had to wait 12 years for her next chance at Olympic gold. By then she was 30 and many people thought she was too old to be a world-class runner. But after having a baby, she came out of retirement and trained hard, taking her baby with her around the stadiums of Europe. In the end she astonished everyone by grabbing gold in four events, including the 100 meter in the speedy time of 11.9 seconds.

KIP KEINO
Nationality: **Kenyan**
Event: **1,500 m**
The 1,500 meter, also known as the mile, requires a brilliant combination of tactics, skill, and incredible stamina. Some of the greatest middle-distance runners have been Kenyans, and at the Mexico City Olympics in 1968, Kenyan Kip Keino raced into the record books. His 1,500-meter win was staggering, due to the fact that on the day of the final Keino was stuck in a terrible traffic jam and had to jog almost a mile to the stadium so he wouldn't miss his big race. Obviously, the jog was a great warm-up for him!

▲ MARITA KOCH
Nationality: **East German**
Event: **400 m**
One athlete who was way ahead of the rest for 12 years was Marita Koch, the incredible East German 400-meter runner. She broke the world record in this event no less than seven times.

LASSE VIREN
Nationality: **Finnish**
Event: **5,000 and 10,000 m**
As a Finnish policeman, Lasse Viren knew how to make an arresting finish! In the Munich Games in 1972 he ran away with gold in both the 5,000 and 10,000 meters. And despite falling on the track in the 10,000 meters, he got up and smashed the world record. Four years later he achieved the double again, when he snatched gold in the same two races at the Montreal Games.

▼ ED MOSES
Nationality: **American**
Event: **400-m hurdles**
No man has ever dominated a sport so completely as American Edwin Moses. At the age of 20 he jumped and sprinted to glory in the 400-meter hurdles at the Montreal Olympics. After that he kept breaking his own record, until the Los Angeles Games when he won an Olympic gold medal for a second time.

SCANDAL!

Wars, disasters, cheats, and shock tactics!

Sometimes it's more than just a defiant gesture. During the Munich Games in 1972, Arab terrorists attacked the living quarters of the Israeli team. Two people were killed and nine others were taken hostage in the most tragic

◀ *The tragic aftermath of the 1972 terrorist attack in Munich*

The Olympics don't always go off without a hitch. Over the years, they've been rocked by all manner of catastrophes, from war and terrorism to some highly illegal cheating.

In ancient Greece, the Olympic Games always took place – no matter what was going on. Even if there was a war raging between the different Greek states, a truce was declared for the period of the Games. But because of the scale of World War I and World War II, during those years the Games were cancelled.

Because of international conflicts, countries have sometimes withdrawn their athletes from the Games. In 1980 the United States refused to turn up at the Moscow Olympics in protest of the Soviet Union's invasion of Afghanistan. Four years later, the USSR boycotted the Los Angeles Games.

◀ *Russian fencer Boris Onischenko was stripped of gold when it was revealed he had tampered with his épée.*

disaster to tarnish Olympic history. After a long gunfight, nine more Israeli athletes, five terrorists, and a German policeman were added to the death toll.

SHOCKING

A scandal that shook the whole world took place on Saturday, September 24, 1988, following the final of the 100 meters in Seoul. The atmosphere in the stadium was electric as the fastest men in the world, including Carl Lewis, Linford Christie (below left), and Ben Johnson (below right) walked out to make Olympic history.

Ben Johnson blasted out of the blocks, smashing the world record in the superhuman time of 9.79 seconds. It was the fastest race in history, and Johnson was declared the fastest man in the world. But not for long. Just a few hours later, tests showed he had taken drugs. He was stripped of his gold medal and returned home to Canada in disgrace.

But he wasn't the first athlete to take drugs, and it's almost certain that he won't be the last. For many, many years drugs have been used to pump up Olympic performances. In 1904 the St. Louis marathon winner Thomas Hicks was given a mixture of drugs and brandy while he was actually running the race. Then in 1960 the Danish cyclist Knut Jensen died in sweltering heat during the Olympic road race in Rome – not of sunstroke, but from a drug overdose.

I'M LATE, I'M LATE!

Some Olympic disasters are just plain silly. The two American 100-meter runners Eddie Hart and Ray Robinson must have been hopping mad when they couldn't compete in the 1972 final. Their bus had an out-of-date timetable – but they were the ones branded as "slow coaches!"

Miruts Yifter from Ethiopia was late for his heat of the 5,000 meters at the 1972 Munich Olympics, when he spent too long in the bathroom. After missing his chance of a medal, he had to wait until 1980 before he could run away with the gold.

WOMAN OR MAN?

In the 1930s Stella Walsh of Poland was one of the world's fastest runners. She snatched the gold medal at the Amsterdam Olympics in 1932 and the silver in Berlin in 1936. However, when she died almost 44 years later, it was discovered that she was actually a man.

I f someone asked you to strap two pieces of metal to your feet and launch yourself off a high mountain, you'd probably think he was crazy. But at the Winter Olympics downhill skiers do just that – and love it! In the downhill event, competitors reach incredible speeds of up to 75 mph! Skiers love the thrill of speed and the sense of danger, but the organizers ensure the course is safe, adding a few twists and turns to slow it down. Even so, the men's downhill race always includes a death-defying 2,600-foot drop!

EVERY SECOND COUNTS

There have been many incredible downhill skiers, but probably the greatest of them all was the Frenchman

❄ ICE ❄ ACES!

There's nothing cooler than the Winter Olympics!

Jean Claude Killy, who skied away with three gold medals at the 1968 Winter Olympics in Grenoble. Another great downhill skier who performed like a turbo-charged meteor was the Austrian Franz Klammer. Although he was trailing in third place after the first half

of the 1976 Innsbruck downhill race, he seemed to fly through the second half and slid away with the gold, winning by just one third of a second.

As well as downhill skiers there are other mega mountain-movers. The slalom and giant slalom

involve the skier moving as fast as possible between poles on a course. The greatest Olympic slalom racer of all time, Alberto Tomba from Italy, has taken home medals from three consecutive Olympics and five medals overall – a record for alpine skiing.

SPEED KINGS

The fastest speeds at any Winter Olympics are reached by the bobsled teams. Hurtling along a tunnel of sheer ice, bobsleds of two or four people reach speeds of 90 mph! And as the bobsleds themselves get more and more technologically advanced, the sport has become very competitive. It's well known that rival teams often spy on each other's equipment to try to get an edge on their opponents' machines.

▲ Speed skating first became popular in the early 1900s and was added to the Olympic lineup in 1924.

TAKE OFF!

One of the most spectacular of all Winter Olympic sports is the ski jump. Jumpers seem to glide through the air like birds. But the skis they wear are much longer and heavier than alpine skis, weighing over 15 lb each.

Jumpers are judged on the quality of their takeoff, plus the landing and the smoothness of their flight through the air. Although it looks dangerous and speeds of 60 mph are often reached, jumping is relatively safe as long as the weather is fine.

One of the greatest ski jumpers in the world is the Finn Matti Nykänen, who won gold at the 1984 and 1988 Winter Olympics. While he was leading the 1988 event, back in last position was Britain's Michael Edwards, nicknamed

Alberto Tomba glides to his gold medal in 1988, while Matti Nykänen soars to his.

Eddie the Eagle. He became famous almost overnight for being just plain bad, scoring less than half the points of any other jumper!

LET'S DANCE!

The most graceful and beautiful winter sport to watch is figure skating. Norway's Sonja Henie was an ice legend who competed in her first games in 1924 when she was just 10 years old. After that she went on to glide for gold in 1928, 1932, and 1936.

Of all the figure skating events, ice dancing is the favorite with the Olympic crowd. Great Britain's Jane

Torvill and Christopher Dean (below) dominated the pairs event for years, and in the 1984 Olympics notched up no less than twelve 6.0 perfect scores. Cool!

Everyone said they were crazy when the Jamaicans sent a bobsled team from one of the hottest places in the world to the 1988 Winter Olympics in Calgary. They were the first team to compete from a Caribbean country – where snowfall is as likely as the sun refusing to shine!

The team had been spotted by their coach at the annual pushcart championships in Kingston, Jamaica. He realized that the technique for pushcarting was similar to bobsledding and convinced the team to compete. Although they didn't come in the running for the medals, and even lost a runner from their sled, they managed to clock a very fast time at the top of the course.

TALKING SHOP

One athlete who was completely flummoxed by her own success was the British 800-meter runner Ann Packer (below). She finished badly in her opening heats of the 1964 Games in Tokyo and was so disappointed with her performance that she was about to put away her running shoes and go

United States athlete Ray Ewry was struck down by polio as a child and spent years on crutches, unable to move his legs properly. However, in 1900, 1904, and 1908, he leaped right into the record books with an amazing eight gold medals for the standing triple jump, standing long jump, and standing high jump.

WE WON!

The underdogs come shining through!

shopping in Tokyo! Luckily she changed her mind and went on to cruise to gold in the 800-meter final.

BELIEVE IN ME

High jumper Duncan McNaughton was determined to compete in the 1932 Olympics, even though he'd been left off the Canadian team. After months of nonstop pestering, he persuaded the Canadian selectors to let him go. No one believed he was good enough to finish in the first ten placings, so he had a big spring in his step when he leaped off with the gold medal!

PILGRIM'S PROGRESS

Many people didn't know his name or where he'd come from as the mystery athlete stood at the 400-meter starting line in Athens in 1906. But after running away with gold in both the 400 and 800 meters, American Paul Pilgrim became a celebrity almost overnight. Unfortunately, he never won a major race again. Oh, dear!

FIGHTING TALK

It's one-to-one action!

GRIPPING STUFF!

Wrestling is one of the oldest Olympic sports, dating back to the ancient Greek Games. Many countries have their own forms of wrestling, but the Olympic events are divided into two categories – freestyle and Greco-Roman.

At the early Games there were no weight categories, so big and small wrestlers battled it out together. Also, there was no time limit – one match in 1912 lasted an exhausting 11 hours and 40 minutes!

ADVANTAGE JAPAN!

Judo was first introduced to the Olympics in 1964 at the request of the host country, Japan. For the Tokyo Games there were four different divisions in the event: lightweight, middleweight, heavyweight, and open class. Needless to say, the Japanese carried off most of the medals in their chosen sport!

ON GUARD!

Just like swashbucklers from Hollywood movies, fencers battle it out with a sword. The object is to score a hit, or "touch," on your opponent with the tip of your blade. Fencing is all about technique and movement, and modern fencers move like dancers around the fencing arena.

BOXING CLEVER!

Boxing is one of the most popular sports at the Olympics, with many gold medalists turning professional and becoming world-class champions. The list of Olympic gold medal winners includes some of the biggest names in the sport, such as Muhammad Ali and Sugar Ray Leonard. However, many people think it's too dangerous to be included in the Games, and in 1912 the Swedes banned boxing from their Olympic lineup.

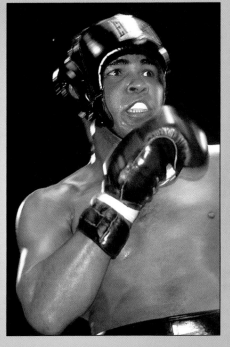

The decathlon: ten times more of a challenge

Every Olympic athlete excels at his or her own sport, but decathletes have to be ten times as good! The decathlon is one of the oldest events in Olympic history, dating back to 708 B.C.

At that time the event was known as the pentathlon and consisted of five events – running, javelin and discus throwing, wrestling, and long-jumping. It was a great honor for the athlete who excelled in the event. As well as being showered with gifts, winners were often treated as if they were superhuman gods!

TOP TEN

The decathlon is a two-day competition that tests stamina and the athletes' ability to shine in ten different events. The word decathlon comes from the Greek words *deka*, meaning ten, and *athlon*, meaning contest. It consists of the 100-meter sprint, long jump, shot put, high jump, and the 400-meter run on the first day. Then the athletes compete in the 110-meter

American decathlete Jim Thorpe finished 700 points ahead of his nearest opponent!

NTS

hurdles, the discus, pole vault, javelin, and 1,500-meter race. Athletes don't need to win every event, but must finish near the top in a high number of sports.

GOLDEN GREATS

In 1912 at the Stockholm Games there was one clear favorite for the decathlon gold. American Jim Thorpe (left) cruised the 10 events, finishing 700 points ahead of his nearest rival! In fact, the King of Sweden, who presented his award, told him, "You, sir, are the greatest athlete in the world." Unfortunately, Jim was stripped of his medal a few years later, when the Olympic Committee learned that he was playing baseball for money. Happily for Jim's family, the decision was reversed after his death.

Bob Mathias, from California, was the youngest track and field gold medalist. At 17 he won the decathlon gold at the London Games in 1948. It was a grueling test of his abilities. His last javelin throw was completed in almost pitch darkness as the light was fading on a dismal London day. The judges even had to use a flashlight to find his javelin on the field!

SUPERMAN DALEY

Probably the greatest decathlete of all time was Great Britain's Daley Thompson (below). In super-human fashion, he won every decathlon he entered, from 1977 to 1984. He grabbed gold at

the 1980 and 1984 Olympics and was all set for a third at Seoul in 1988, but tragically his pole snapped and he was badly injured.

Always a bit of a joker, Daley Thompson once described the decathlon as "Nine Mickey Mouse events and 1,500 meters."

MOVE OVER, DALEY!

American decathlete Dan O'Brien narrowly missed his chance to compete in the 1992 Olympics, failing to qualify in the pole-vaulting event. In 1995 he went on to smash the world record for decathlon points in Gothenburg, and the hot tips say he may be the next Daley Thompson.

HEP TO IT!

Until 1984 the ancient Greek format of the five-event pentathlon was kept for women. This was then changed to the seven-event heptathlon to add two more tests. Of all the heptathlon and pentathlon successes, American Jackie Joyner-Kersee stands out. In 1984 she missed winning the gold by five points when Australian Glynnis Nunn won the first heptathlon. Determined to win, Joyner-Kersee trained hard for the Seoul Olympics and sped home with a world record score of 7,291 points. She was a clear 394 points in front of the silver medalist.

ALL FOR ONE
and one for all!

Winning team tactics

▲ *Poland and Spain go for golden goals in 1992.*

Team sports have **been part of the Olympics since the beginning of the century.** Track and field and gymnastics are probably the most popular, but there have been many magical moments in other team sports, such as hockey and soccer.

Until recently, professional soccer players weren't allowed to compete in the Olympics because of its amateur status. But in 1984 this rule was changed, moving the goalposts forward for the future of the sport.

Now that professional stars can get into the action, the Olympics would seem to be able to compete with the competition and drama of the World Cup.
But even though the new rule has come into play, the world's most famous teams still aren't netting the medals.

One of the biggest surprises took place at the Seoul Olympics in 1988 when an unknown team, Zambia, beat the world class Italians with a 4-0 win in the first round!

TALL STORY

If it's high drama you're after, then look no farther than the Olympic basketball court. Here some of the tallest men in the world jostle for net supremacy.

The first basketball match was played out at the Berlin Olympics in 1936. During the tournament the International Basketball Federation tried to ban any players taller than 6 feet 3 inches from the Games. This tall order sparked a wave of protest from the U.S. giants, and luckily the silly height rule was withdrawn.

But big doesn't always mean better. At the 1948 Games in London, the U.S. team was up against the Chinese team, which had some of the smallest players in the competition. One of the Chinese players was having trouble getting around Bob Kurland, the 7-foot U.S. center player – so he decided to run between his legs and went on to score! Slam-dunk!

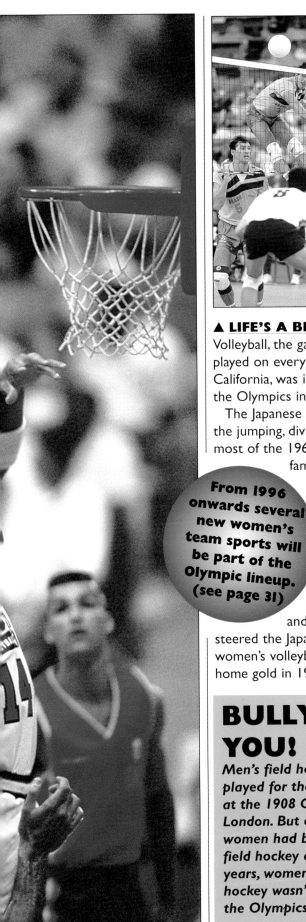

▲ LIFE'S A BEACH

Volleyball, the game that's played on every beach in California, was introduced to the Olympics in 1964.

The Japanese dominated the jumping, diving game for most of the 1960s. One famous coach, Hirofumi Diamatsu, trained his players six hours a day, seven days a week, and eventually steered the Japanese women's volleyball team to home gold in 1964.

From 1996 onwards several new women's team sports will be part of the Olympic lineup. (see page 31)

VERY HANDY!

Mix basketball and soccer together and what do you get? Handball, that's what. It's been an Olympic sport since 1972 and is played by a team of six players plus a goalkeeper on each side. In handball the ball is passed down the field by hands instead of feet. Then, instead of being thrown through a hoop like basketball, it's thrown past the goalie into a net. It's a great sport for natural soccer foulers!

BULLY FOR YOU!

Men's field hockey was played for the first time at the 1908 Games in London. But even though women had been playing field hockey at school for years, women's field hockey wasn't added to the Olympics until 1980.

WATER WAY *to win*

The spills and thrills of Olympic water events

Believe it or not, the first Olympic swimming championships weren't held in a clean, warm swimming pool but in the sea! In fact, competitors in the 1,500-meter freestyle event in Athens in 1896 had to struggle with freezing cold water and 12-foot waves. Alfred Hajos, who eventually won the race, had to cover his body in an inch of grease to help keep himself warm – it was a question of survival rather than winning.

Champion swimmer Dawn Fraser (below, center) led a pretty eventful life in and out of the water. Despite a terrible car crash in February 1964, which killed her mother and left her with cracked vertebrae and her neck in a cast, a few months later she went on to win the 100-meter freestyle gold medal at the Tokyo Olympics. However, she got herself into hot water when she stole a flag from the Japanese emperor's palace as a dare and was suspended by the Australian team. Nevertheless she ended up dripping in Olympic medals – four silver and four gold.

▲ WINNING TACTICS

At school British swimmer Duncan Goodhew had been teased by his classmates because he was dyslexic and had lost all his hair in an accident. But he had the last laugh when he won gold for the 100-meter breaststroke at the 1980 games in Moscow.

Being hairless had its advantages, too. While the other swimmers had to shave their bodies to make themselves as streamlined as possible, Duncan could relax and put his feet up.

Canadian Sylvie Bernier, who won the women's springboard diving in 1984, had a different way of relaxing before a big race. She had terrible problems with nerves, so she shut out the sound of the stadium by

calmly listening to music on her Walkman before diving for the medals.

TALES OF THE UNEXPECTED

Winning isn't always the top priority. Some Olympic events have turned into a battle for survival!

Lawrence Lemieux, from Canada, was in second place in the fifth race of the Finn Class yachting event at the 1988 Olympics in Seoul. Suddenly he

White-water slalom racing was first introduced to the Olympics at the Munich Games in 1972. It was won easily by the East Germans, who had built an exact copy of the course so they could practice before the Games!

noticed another competitor from Singapore struggling in the water with his capsized boat. Lemieux turned his boat around and saved him. Although he didn't win an Olympic medal, Lemieux was given a special award for gallantry.

In Melbourne in 1956, Stuart Mackenzie, from Australia, looked all set to row away with the single sculls gold. But suddenly, as if from nowhere, 18-year-old Vyacheslav Ivanov, from the Soviet Union, put on an incredible spurt of speed and snatched the gold. Ivanov was so excited by his win that he jumped up and down for joy on the winner's rostrum and dropped his medal in the nearby lake. He immediately dived in to retrieve it, but to no avail. Luckily, the committee agreed to give him a replacement medal.

The first horses and riders pranced into the Olympics at the Stockholm Games in 1912. Since then, equestrian events have become one of the highlights of the Games.

Equestrian games are divided into three sections – three-day eventing, jumping, and dressage. For each event there are medals for the best team and the best rider.

Three-day eventing is the most testing of all the equestrian competitions. In it, the horse and rider have to complete a grueling long-distance obstacle course, perform a series of set movements called dressage, and compete in show-jumping.

To ride away with Olympic gold at three-day eventing is a great achievement. Riders often fall or are not able to complete the hazardous obstacle course, which includes deep-water jumps and riding cross-country. So to win gold twice in succession is almost unheard of. Only two people have done this in the history of equestrian Olympics – Charles Pahud de Mortanges on his horse Marcroix in 1928 and 1932 and the incredible Mark Todd from New Zealand on Charisma in 1984 and 1988.

HIGH STAKES

Like some other Olympic events, riding is an amateur sport, but it's a very costly business. Competitors not only have to raise the money to find and train the

HORSING AROUND

Saddle up for equestrian action!

▲ *Three-day eventing, the most testing of the equestrian events*

In 1968 in Mexico, two horses died of exhaustion on the obstacle course, and only half the competitors finished.

right horse, but also transport it with all the necessary equipment to the Games. Many competitors have had to sell their homes and possessions in order to raise the money. Mark Todd was a cattle farmer in New Zealand. He sold most of his herd to enable him to make his life-long Olympic dream come true.

TRAGEDY STRIKES

As well as the financial gamble, riding can be dangerous and sometimes tragic. Horses occasionally die in the Olympics, and riders have broken limbs while attempting the demanding events. The obstacle course at the Berlin Olympics in 1936 was so difficult that three horses died, and only 27 out of the 50 competitors managed to finish.

It was only after an amazing act of bravery that the German team won the team gold at the Berlin Olympics in 1936. One of their three riders, Konrad Freiherr von Wangenheim, fell off his horse, Kurfürst, during the obstacle course and broke his collarbone.

The next day he rode into the arena for the show-jumping event with his arm in a sling. At the double jump, Kurfürst reared up and fell backward onto his stunned rider. Luckily, both the horse and Von Wangenheim were unhurt

▲ *Andrew Nicholson makes a big splash on Spinning Rhombo at the 1992 Barcelona Olympics.*

and went on to complete the course without another fault. They received a standing ovation from the crowd.

GOLDEN HOPES

Another rider who was determined not to let her team down under any circumstances was Karen Stives of the United States. As she and Ben Arthur entered the jumping arena at the 1984 Los Angeles Olympics, they knew that the hopes of the rest of the team and the whole nation were riding on them.

To win team and individual gold she had to clear all 12 jumps without a fault. If she knocked over two fences or more the team gold would go to Great Britain; if she knocked over

Women first competed in the Olympic three-day eventing at the Tokyo Games in 1964.

▲ *American Karen Stives riding Ben Arthur*

one fence Mark Todd would win the individual gold. She jumped ten fences as easily as flying, but with the finish in sight her horse scraped the top of the middle fence and sent the pole clattering to the ground. She won the day for her team but lost the gold to Mark Todd.

▲ *New Zealand's Mark Todd celebrates gold.*

HEAVY!

It may look as though it is just a question of brute strength, but heavyweight sports such as shot-putting, weight lifting, and hammer-throwing require great skill.

▼ HOT SHOTS!
The shot put is one of the most difficult sports of the whole Games. The object of the sport is to "put" the shot (a heavy solid metal ball) as far as possible, by throwing it without stepping outside of a special ring.

SISTER ACT
Two sisters, Irina and Tamara Press (above) from the Soviet Union, both won gold at the 1960 Rome Olympics. They were the first sisters to take home gold in the same year.

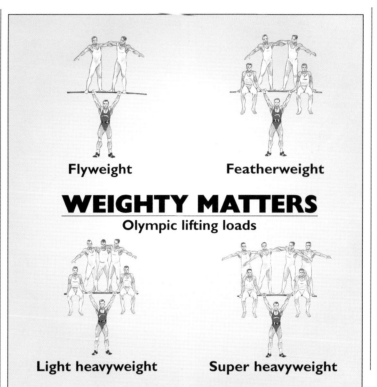

Flyweight   Featherweight

WEIGHTY MATTERS
Olympic lifting loads

Light heavyweight   Super heavyweight

HAMMER TIME!
The hammer is a 15.87-lb metal ball attached to 47.8 inches of steel wire that's hurled as far as possible. When the game was first played in early Olympic competitions in this century, many of the throws ended up in the trees.

One of the greatest hammer-throwers of all time was an American policeman named John Flanagan, who won four gold medals in consecutive Olympics. At 41 he became the oldest record-breaker in track and field history.

▶ POWER RANGERS!
The sport of weight lifting has always been an Olympic event. Year after year,

records are broken as techniques improve. But not all weight lifters are

Modern weight lifting is adapted from 19th century circus stunts.

heavyweight power houses.

The event is divided into different classes depending on the weight of the contestant, with bantamweight and flyweight at the slender end of the scale. American Joe di Pietro, who competed at the London Olympics in 1948, was only 4 feet 8 inches tall. His arms were so short that he could hardly lift the bar over his head!

Believe it or not, the event is as much about weight watching as lifting. The rules say that if two contestants have lifted the same weight, the contestant who weighs in lighter wins. This means that a sneaky snack before a lift could make the difference between winning and losing – or even being able to compete at all!

In the Melbourne Games in 1956 pint-sized American powerlifter Charles Vinci weighed in at about a pound more than was allowed. But he was able to compete after an hour of running in place and a last-minute haircut! What a close shave!

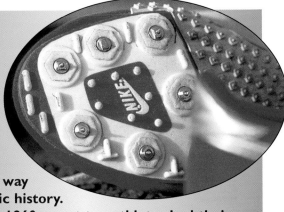

BOOTS ARE MADE FOR RUNNING

The track shoe, the essential footwear of all track athletes, has come a long way in its Olympic history.

Before the 1960s most top athletes had their track shoes made to measure. They would simply take a piece of paper and draw around their foot to get the shape of the foot exactly right. The shoes were often made of hard-wearing kangaroo skin with soft leather uppers and were so well-made that they could last an athlete a lifetime.

Today, however, most athletes wear track shoes made by the company that sponsors them. They can have as many as 100 different pairs and may even slip on a new pair for each race.

On July 29, 1992, at the Barcelona Games, all eyes were on one man and his machine.

Chris Boardman sped home to victory in the final of the 4,000-meter cycle pursuit in a world-record time of 4 minutes 27.357 seconds.

No one had ever seen anything like his Lotus-Sport racing bike with its sleek lines and aerodynamic structure. It was made entirely of lightweight carbon fiber, and unlike other interlocking-tube racing bikes, Lotus-Sport was molded from a single structure. This meant it was much lighter and less wind-resistant. The handlebars on Chris's amazing machine were much lower, too, making it even more aerodynamic. It almost flew to gold!

FASTER THAN THE WIND

When they're skiing down icy mountains at speeds of over 85 mph, skiers have to be sure they have the fastest and safest equipment on the slopes. Downhill and speed skis have to be both streamlined and strong. They are well over six feet long and made of lightweight fiberglass. The tips at the end are flatter than on ordinary skis to give maximum speed and stability and minimum air resistance. The Lycra suits, slick helmets, and curved ski sticks add to the streamlined effect.

SLICE OF ICE

Today's bulletlike bobsleds are sleek, streamlined machines, with steel runners to cut through ice like a knife through butter. Their superlight fiberglass shells have come a long way since their forerunners.

In the early days of the event, bobsleds were made of heavy sheet metal, wood, and even wicker!

MEGA MACHINES

When you're going for gold, equipment plays a vital part

SPORTS FOR ALL

Paralympian action

Immediately after the main **Olympic Games have finished, paralympian athletes get set to go for gold.** The Paralympics were the brainchild of one man, Dr. Ludwig Guttman, who worked at the special hospital for the disabled in Birmingham, England.

For years Dr. Guttman had been treating people who had been left disabled after World War II. He encouraged patients to take up a sport to help them feel active and competitive again, and started holding competitions at the hospital.

The games quickly caught on, and in 1948 the first national Paralympics were held for British athletes only. Soon other countries were clamoring to take part, and by 1992, 3,500 athletes were competing from 82 different countries around the world.

NO LIMITS
To begin with, the longest race was just 60 yards, as anything longer was considered too difficult for the athletes. But by 1984 athletes with disabilities were competing in mega marathons and finishing in under two hours.

The standard of athletic ability at the Paralympics is incredibly high. Many of the sports are the same as those at the Olympics, such as swimming and athletics, and some are adapted, depending on the

athlete's disability. Blind soccer players play goalball rather than soccer, with a ball containing bells that is rolled along the playing field rather than kicked into the air.

Technology has also helped to open up sports to people with disabilities. Wheelchairs are custom-built for racing, with lightweight aluminum frames, bucket seats, and special wheels. In shooting, the gun-sight is linked to a computer that sends out different tones depending on the section of the target that the gun is pointing at.

Tanni Grey from Britain is one of the megastars of the wheelchair track. At the Barcelona Paralympics in 1992 she sped away with four gold medals and smashed two world and two Paralympic records.

THE WAY FORWARD

New challenges for tomorrow's Olympians

Along with the all-time favorites, new sports and events are tried out each Olympic year.

Some traditional sports, like marathon running and gymnastics, will always be part of the Olympic agenda, but new events such as surfing and ballroom dancing have gold in their sights.

New sports often start out as "demonstration" events. They're not part of the official Games and there are no medals up for grabs. These demonstration events have been a feature of the Olympics since 1904 and are usually chosen by the host country.

Ultimately, only a small proportion of the sports are actually added to the Olympic agenda. Most, such as dog-sledding and waterskiing, don't make it as serious contenders. The three newest Olympic sports swung into action at the Barcelona games in 1992. These were women's windsurfing, women's judo, and the reinstated canoe slalom.

GETTING IN THE SWIM

In order to get selected, the organization representing a sport has to make a special presentation to the governing body of the Olympics – the International Olympic Committee. If it's popular enough, the sport is then voted into the Games.

For several years synchronized swimmers tried to become part of the Olympics, and in 1984 they were finally allowed to dip a toe in the water. Although many people claimed that it wasn't a real sport, synchronized swimming has become very popular because of the agility required and the glamor of the event.

RETURN MATCH

Tennis was popular in the early games up until the Paris Olympics in 1924. After that it wasn't played again until 1988. The sport was very popular with the early host countries, but later host countries didn't have enough good tennis players and so it was phased out.

Luckily, it was served up again at the 1988 Olympics in Seoul and has returned as one of the most popular events, with all the top players taking part.

Maybe one day, other discontinued sports, such as rugby, will return to the greatest international competition in the world. As for croquet, that's a little less likely!

HELLO, GOODBYE

The sports that are hoping to be part of the Olympic lineup and the ones that have been discontinued:

IN

Women's triple jump
Badminton mixed
 doubles
Beach volleyball
Mountain biking
Women's soccer
Rhythmic gymnastics
 women's team event

OUT

Golf
Motor boating
Tug of war
Rugby
Cricket
Croquet

INDEX